MENTAL FIGHT

Ben Okri was born in Minna, Nigeria. His childhood was divided between Nigeria, where he saw first hand the consequences of war, and London. He has won many prizes over the years for his fiction, and is also an acclaimed essayist, playwright, and poet. In 2019 *Astonishing the Gods* was named as one of the BBC's '100 Novels That Shaped Our World'.

Also by Ben Okri

FICTION

Flowers and Shadows
The Landscapes Within
Incidents at the Shrine
Stars of the New Curfew
The Famished Road
Songs of Enchantment
Astonishing the Gods
Dangerous Love
Infinite Riches
In Arcadia
Starbook
The Comic Destiny (previously *Tales of Freedom*)
The Age of Magic
The Magic Lamp
The Freedom Artist
Prayer for the Living

ESSAYS

Birds of Heaven
A Way of Being Free
The Mystery Feast
A Time for New Dreams

POETRY

An African Elegy
Wild
Rise Like Lions (Anthology)
A Fire in My Head

PLAYS

The Outsider

MENTAL FIGHT

An Anthem for the
Twenty-First Century

BEN OKRI

HEAD
ZEUS

An Apollo Book

Mental Fight is based on 'A Moment in Timelessness', first delivered as the inaugural millennium lecture sponsored by the *Scotsman* at the 1997 Edinburgh Book Festival. In its present form, the first two sections were first published in *The Times* in January 1999.

First published in the UK in 1999 by Phoenix House.
This revised edition published in the UK in 2021 by Head of Zeus Ltd,
This paperpack edition first published in the UK in 2022 by Head of Zeus Ltd,
part of Bloomsbury Publishing Plc

9 7 5 3 1 2 4 6 8

A catalogue record for this book is available from
the British Library.

ISBN (PB): 9781800244269
ISBN (E): 9781800244245

Typeset by Adrian McLaughlin

Printed and bound in Great Britain by
CPI Group (UK) Ltd, Croydon CR0 4YY

Head of Zeus Ltd
First Floor East
5–8 Hardwick Street
London EC1R 4RG

WWW.HEADOFZEUS.COM

To Humanity in the Aquarian Age

I will not cease from Mental Fight
Nor shall my sword sleep in my hand
Till we have built Jerusalem

William Blake

ONE

Time to be real

I

An illusion by which we can
Become more real.
A moment unremarked
By the universe,
By nature, the seasons, or stars.
Moment we have marked out
In timelessness.
Human moment.
Making a ritual, a drama, a tear
On eternity. Domesticating
The infinite.
Contemplating quantum questions:
Time, death, new beginnings,
Regeneration, cycles, the unknown.

II

Let uncontemplated regions
Of time project themselves
Into your sleeping consciousness,
Inducing terror, or mental liberation.
So death-confrontation
Paralyses some with despair
And makes others poison
Themselves with emptiness
But releases in a fortunate few
A rare quality of enlightenment,
A sense of the limited time we have
Here on earth to live magnificently
To be as great and happy as we can
To explore our potentials beyond the limits
To lose our fear of death
Having gained greater love
And reverence for life,
Its incommensurable golden brevity.

That's how it is
With this moment.
Gigantic death
Enormous birth.
Mighty moment
In timelessness.

III

Illusions are useful only if we use them
To help us get to our true reality.
Initiations and rituals, if they're noble,
Have this power,
(They magnify the secret hour)
They help us to pass from
The illusion of lesser selves
To the reality of our greater selves,
To our soaring powers.
They free us from smallness,
'Our humiliated consciousness,' as Camus wrote,
And they deliver us
Back into what we really are
What we sometimes suspect we are
What we glimpse we are when we are in love,
Magnificent and mysterious
Beings, capable of creating civilisations
Out of the wild lands of the earth,
And the dark places in our consciousness.

In ways small and great, we're
The figures, the myths and legends
That we ourselves have invented.
Our dreams are self-portraits.
Our myths, our heroic legends,
Are the concealed autobiography

Of the human race,
Its struggles through
Darkness to light
And through higher
Darkness again.

IV

Human kind cannot live
For long
With the notion
Or the reality
Of timelessness.
Only in mind.
Only in the spirit.

With us, things must
Have a beginning. For
Theatre grew from ritual
And ritual grew
Out of silence.
Here, now, an origin.
We're poised always
At the threshold
Of an unknown,
Unwritten, and
Unforeseen act.

O Let's gather
Ourselves
Together, clear
Our minds,
Be present to
Ourselves

And to our age.
Focussed
On this stage.
That we
Concentrate. And listen.
That we prepare
Ourselves
In seriousness
And joy.
Let's be wonderfully
Awake
For what we are going
To create,
To make happen,
In this mass co-scripting
Of the future.

V

Now is a material event.
It is also a spiritual moment.
The blinding light of the real can
Pierce through and tear
Asunder the unreal.
Every moment carries
The ordinary and monumental:
Staring out of a grey office window
Or being blinded, like Paul
On the blue road to Damascus
By the light of true seeing.
Then the celluloid of what seems
Like the real world
Is stripped away.
And behind it all we see things
As they could be.
A better world,
A world renewed.

That's what this moment is.
It carries dust and dreams
Pavement or streams.
A moment on the clock
Or a moment of the spirit.
I dream of what it can be,
I dream of what this millennial

Moment can be,
What we could let it be:
A wonderful excuse for beginning
A clearing out of the garbage
In our histories, our consciousness.
Best excuse in a thousand years
To transcend our grim ancient fears

VI

Everyone loves a spring cleaning.
Let's have humanity cleaning.
Open up history's chamber of horrors
And clear out the skeletons behind the mirrors,
Put our breeding nightmares to flight
Transform our monsters with our light.
Clean the stables
In our celebrated fables
A gigantic cleaning
Is no mean undertaking.
A cleaning of pogroms and fears
Of genocide and tears
Of torture and slavery
Of hatred and brutality.
Let us turn around and face them
Let us turn around and face them
Bullies that our pasts have become
Let us turn around and face them
Let's make this clearing out moment
A legendary material atonement.

TWO

Signs from the old times

I

O the hallucinations that fall upon you
When you resist revelation,
When you resist epiphanies,
And when you close yourself
Off from enlightenment.
The opposite of a spiritual dawn
Is a universal nightmare.
Then the mind multiplies
The illusion of things
Till they become not gods,
But the god-like monsters.

O the nightmare visions
Of Breughel and of Bosch,
The infernos of drug-addicts,
The neurotic hades
Are but the mental productions
Of illusions gone wrong.
Apocalyptic visions are of great value.
They show us what the world
Will be like if we don't
Open ourselves to the other side,
To light, to freed thinking.
They are moral signposts
On the way to hell.

II

What will we choose?
Will we allow ourselves descend
Into universal chaos and darkness?
A world without hope, and without wholeness
Without moorings, and without light
Without the possibility for mental fight,
A world breeding mass murderers
Energy vampires, serial killers
With minds spinning in anomie and amorality
With murder, rape, genocide as normality?
Will we allow ourselves merely to drift
Into an era of more of the same
An era drained of significance, without shame,
Without wonder, or excitement,
With just the same low-grade entertainment,
An era boring and predictable
'Flat, stale, weary, and unprofitable'
In which we drift
In which we drift along
Too bored and too passive to care
About what strange realities rear
Their heads in our days and our nights,
Till we awake too late to the death of our rights
Too late to do anything, too
Late for thinking
About what we've allowed

To take over our lives
As we cruised along in casual flight
Mildly indifferent to storm or to sunlight?

III

Or might we choose to make
This time a waking-up event
A moment of true world empowerment?
To pledge, in private, to be more aware
More playful, more tolerant, and more fair
More responsible, more wild, more loving
Awake to our unsuspected powers, more amazing.

We rise or fall by the choice we make
It all depends on the road we take
And the choice and the road depend
On the light we have, the light we bend,
The light we use
Or refuse
On the lies we live by
From which we die.

IV

Every moment bears the monumental
In the ordinary,
Transcending the political
Hinting at the evolutionary.

Great sudden leaps of consciousness,
The spontaneous descent into atavism
Might seem revolutionary
But they're merely the seeds,
Long hidden in the earth,
Bursting forth into shoot.
They're merely the moments
In which what was hidden
Growing unseen in history's depths,
Suddenly combusts, bringing forth
Its truest forms,
And revealing its real nature.
The speed and suddenness
Of an appearance
Is really only that moment
When we become aware
Of the change in a condition
(As in an enchanter's invocation)
A change that'd been changing
All along, without our being aware of it.

V

So under the powerful sun
And fertile intensity of this great moment
Many thoughts, forms, philosophies,
Regressions, advancements, and tendencies,
Many hybrids, fusions, and contortions,
And startling, sinister conversations
Will pour out noisily
From the weird oracles of humanity.
A tidal wave of them.
Many things, many signs
From the old times
Speed forth to fruition
Born too quickly
Too violently, too silently
The world aquiver with peculiar spawns
Born into early sunlight and harsh dawns.

And there would be
Too many gods
And too many Delphis
An unholy babbling
All over the narrow spaces.

Everywhere an excess of dreams,
Of forebodings, art forms,
Of rituals, ways, and interpretations,

Of roads, signs and wonders,
Of prognostications, wayward visions.
Babel is rebuilt among us.
Babel's reborn.

VI

We know only
Two kinds of response
To the unknown.
Awe – noise;
Silence – terror;
Humility – paralysis;
Prayer – panic;
Stillness, or speech;
Watchfulness – myth-making;
Seeing clearly, or inventing what we see;
Standing – fleeing;
Reasoning, or falling apart;
Courage, or cowardice.

The unknown lives with us,
And lives in each moment.
Like a new millennium,
The unknown remains as
Richly potent
As the critical mass
Of our mass minds
Facing the momentous.

Humanity is at
Its most radioactive.
Fusing and fissioning.
Radiating abundant energies

Like so many little solar systems.
Hurling out profusions of seeds,
Like the fertile season
In great forests.
Out of these energies,
And out of time's sifting,
Will come a new future
That's unrecognisable to
Those of us who
Live and breathe now.

Out of so many seeds,
(Innumerable deeds,)
Will come a new humanity
Which will owe much
To this point of the cusp,
To this moment in which we live,
To now, here, as we move
Towards the flowing future time
That's bearing us ever onwards
Into eternity.

We're the best placed farmers
Of new time. We're
At a precious moment
In time's ovulation.

We are now at that rare intersection
That magic favours, that
History adores,
That legend has no need to embellish
Because it is already a legendary moment
In its own wonderful right.

VII

How often have great minds
In the past prayed and wished for
Better favoured moments
In time to unleash their highest
Gifts on humanity? This
Is one such conjunction:
It fills the heart with much
Humility and amazement
To behold. But we must
Behold it, with minds calm,
With aspirations clear,
And with the smile in the soul
That only those fortunate people have
Who find themselves in the right time,
The perfect mythic conjunction,
That is also a living moment. A
Moment lived through.

We're living in enchanted time.
With our spirits right we
Can enchant the future.
With our love's might
We can give a truer
Meaning to our past.

THREE

Is humanity exhausted?

I

Is time exhausted? No,
Time is yet young
And has endless
Millennia ahead, way
Beyond our furthest dreams.

Is nature exhausted? Ask
The bristlecone pines, the hollies,
The flowers, birds, fishes, and lions.
They will continue for as long
As the earth allows them.

And is humanity exhausted?
Individuals are, nations are,
And some civilisations are becoming so.
But humanity isn't.

Hungry nations are hungry still.
The starving people dream of food.
The unfree fight for their freedom.
The oppressed plan for real liberation.
The small struggle for might.
The invisible strive for higher visibility.

They are only exhausted
Who think they are.

They are only exhausted who no longer
Have a reason to strive
And dream and hope.

They are only exhausted who think
They have arrived
At their final destination,
The end of their own road,
With all their dreams achieved,
And no new dreams to hold.

The exhausted are those who have
Come to the end of their powers
Of imagination, who've limited
Their possibilities, who've thought
Themselves to the dead ends
That they call the highest
Points of their civilisations.

Those who're exhausted have
Lost the greater picture,
The greater perspective.
They're trapped in their own labyrinth,
Their lovelessness, and selfishness.
For those with narrow dreams,
There is chaos to come.
Disintegration. And nightmares.

I hear them talk about the end
Of history. But
Those of us who have not tasted
The best fruits of time yet, to
Whom history has been harsh,
We think differently.
We know that history's all
There to be made in the future.

Exhaustion is a mental thing,
The absence of a spiritual viewpoint,
And a universal vision,
A sense of new journeys,
Higher discoveries.

There is no exhaustion
Where there is much
To be hoped for,
To work towards,
And where the dreams
And sufferings
Of our ancestors
Have not been realised,
Redeemed.

There's no exhaustion when
You can still visualise

A better life for people who suffer;
When you can visualise
Universal justice;
A leavening of the great dough
Of humanity. Uplifting
The multitudes.

But when you can no longer dream
No longer see the possibilities
No longer see alternatives;
When you can see only limitation,
Despair, and negation,
Then you are in the way.
You're also the problem.
The exhausted obstruct
The creation of a greater future.

The exhausted should therefore clear
The stage for new dreamers –
For warriors of love, justice,
Enlightenment.

II

Have all thoughts, possibilities, ideas,
Philosophies been exhausted?
Has Christianity found its fullest
Fruition in great cathedrals, charities,
Schisms, wars, divisions, orthodoxies,
And sundry creeds?
I do not believe that Christianity
Has yet yielded ailing humanity
Its best fruits. Unrealised remain
Her fullest possibilities.

Have Buddhism, Taoism, or Hinduism,
Islam, Humanism and Existentialism,
All the spiritual aspirations of the race
All thoughts of social organisation,
ideas technological and scientific –
Have they all been richly realised,
Fully mined, made to serve,
Ennoble and feed humankind?
I don't think so either.
Look at history; see what you find.

FOUR

The stony ground

I

Humanity has been so much like a child
With too many rich, useful toys,
Playing with each one that's given,
And discarding it when something
Newer appears in its midst.

We have been dilettantes and amateurs
With some of our greatest notions
For human betterment.
We have been spoilt children:
We have been like tyrannical children;
Impatient and imperious, demanding
Proof when listening is required,
Tearing things down when they don't do
What we want them to do
(How much simpler to let things do only
What they can do)
Being uncreative about what seems dark
And terrifying; preferring
Only what seems easy
And effortless;
Questioning the numbers
Of a philosophy's
Followers rather than examining
The fruitfulness of its ideas;
Wandering down blind alleys of populism

That lead to concentration camps;
Refusing to admit our vast crimes and mistakes
Denying the horrors of the slave trade
Minimising the reality of the gas chambers
Tearing our hair out in futile attempts
At reconciling civilisation with genocide,
When civilisation (as we have come to accept it)
Never did mean the true universal goodness
Of heart, but rather meant the self-mythology
Of a people, a race.
No, neither the good in us, nor
Our capacity for evil are exhausted.
Time will show just how young
We are in our abilities,
Our genius for good and evil.
For all these strains, unexamined,
And unredeemed,
Will find their higher fruition
In the unlit centuries to come.

*   *   *

We carry with us, across the silver river
Of the new age, many ambiguous
And deadly seeds,
And also many seeds of illumination.

We are the sum total of the history
That we've not truly examined.
We are the carriers of history's
Future diseases or their cures.
The sooner we face the spawn we
Carry within us in silence
The better it will be.
The sooner we admit our crimes
To others – to other peoples, genders,
Species, creeds – the better
And lighter the human
Future will be.
The more we deny, the greater
Will then be the horrors
And vengeances of time
That wait silently in the wings
Of the bloody drama of our future.

Many beautiful thoughts
Have not yet sprouted in
Our deepest hearts and minds,
Though they have lain there, within us,
Lain waiting for thousands of years.
The heart of humanity can
Sometimes be a stony
Ground indeed. We

Speak the good words,
But don't live them;
Perform the beautiful rituals,
But don't embody them.
We praise our capacity for reason,
But remain unreasonably intolerant
Of other people's validity, and reasons.
And we deploy the finest attributes
Of the mind and spirit
To make of ourselves the elect,
Then cast our fellow travellers
On earth into outer darkness.

What a wonder is humanity: how
Marvellous its astonishing
Gift for hypocrisy.

II

How healthy is the human race?
When the foot is swollen, the kidney ailing,
The neck stiff, the spirit troubled,
The heart irregular, the head stuffy,
The thoughts narrow and negative,
But the whole taken together
Generally quite functional,
Can we say that the body is healthy?
So it is with humanity.

Here're some of the illnesses of the race:
Tyranny and starvation, religious and tribal wars,
Repression, poverty, alienation, indifference,
Genocide, xenophobia, illiteracy,
Bad governments, epidemics, and selfishness.
We must face the fact that
Given the whole picture
The human race is not that well.

We have also, it cannot be denied,
Accomplished great feats. We've
Journeyed to space and spied on
The solitude of uninhabited planets.
We've created mighty secular
And religious structures,
Made fabulous technological inventions,

Found cures for nasty diseases,
Solved some riddles of human genetics,
Probed the mysteries of the weather,
Shed light on aberrations of the mind,
Unleashed the possibilities of communications,
And tapped the awesome ambiguous
Power of nuclear energy.

Yet because of our pollutions,
Earth's fragile balance is askew.
Humanity dies in refugee camps,
Goes mad in slums,
Is brutalised by evil governments,
Perishes in festering wars.

Yet hatred boils away
For reasons of history
And for different interpretations
Of the same sacred texts
That teach us universal love.

We are amazing: so
Much gold has been revealed
In the human spirit.
So many wonderful philosophies
Of such startling simplicity

Have been dreamt up and shared
Amongst us, and yet we still live
As if in Plato's cave,
Watching shadows
Of suffering go past
As if they had nothing to do with us.
And yet we live as if these thoughts,
These dreams, and these philosophies,
Had never been written,
And never been beneficial.

I contend that the human race
Has not yet reached
The true exalted condition
Of civilisation.

Sure, the quality of life's been enriched
For many over the past centuries;
But true civilisation is much more
Than the financial
And technological progress
Or the well-being of parts
Of the human race.

What we've called civilisations
Are merely stages on the way
To true world civilisation.

FIVE

Harmony of politics and heart

I

Mastery of material problems:
No spiritual way can
Reconcile itself truthfully
With the raw wound
Of starving multitudes.
We can't use the word civilisation
As long as people die of starvation.
Those who do are
Cave-dwellers of the mind.

Transmutation of world-wide poverty
Must become the greatest alchemical
Feat of the dreaming age.
A basic pre-condition of civilisation
Is a world free of hunger.
Cannot be done by charity alone.
Symphony of the rich and poor
Nations of the earth.
No them and us.
No self-satisfaction.
No superiority-thinking.
Just harmony of politics and heart.
The rhythms of economics and art.
Improvisations on themes of justice:
If the rich exploit the poor
We are talking about cannibalism.

If the rich ignore the poor
Absolute violence will be the music
To such deafness.

II

But with all our vaunted glories
We are still largely humiliated
Beings on earth. It's
Time we turned our formidable
Powers of heart and mind
To humanity's solvable problems –
Problems which have become accusations.

III

This earth is our brief home.
Let us put the human house in order
Let us tend the wild garden of humanity.
We're better than the sum total
Of our successes and failures.
The truth's that we
haven't really tried,
haven't really gone for it,
We haven't really striven
For a world of balance
And contentment.
We're like athletes who have
Not really extended themselves.
We haven't found out what we're
Really capable of doing
If we just put our minds to it.
We're functioning below
Our potential for love,
Justice, and creating a good world.

SIX

Hold on to your sanity

I

At the end of powerful eras,
And at the birth of new
Ones, strange spirits spew up
In the world, and in nature,
In the heavens, from our minds.
Turbulences rise from secret places
And from underworlds of history,
From our guilt and denial,
From our wickedness and silence.
From the oppressed
And the suppressed.
From our conscience. Great cries
And monstrous visions sound
From humanity's forgotten
Oracles. Visions of terminal
Horrors and eruptions.

The force of new eras
Clashing with the old,
Like two seas with
Two contending
Powerful gods, unleash
Realities strange to behold.
Collapsing structures multiply:
Superstitions and anomie,
Paranoia and mindless cults,

Conspiracy theories and supernatural
Terrors, suicides, murders,
Wars and fears and panic
Wreak havoc on the world.
Only those with substance,
Whose souls are earthed,
Whose eyes are clear,
Withstand it all.
They pay an awkward price
For such clear-sightedness.
For they will be alone,
But hopefully not as tragically
Alone as the noble family
In Fellini's 'Satyricon' who, unable
To bear such sanity
Amidst universal insanity,
Then elect for stoic suicide.

So watch your minds.
Cling on to the soundest values.
These are severely testing times ahead,
More testing for the sane
Than for those perfectly in tune
With erupting contemporary anomie.

II

For we are living on the cusp
Of wonders and terrors.
Weird tensions flow beneath the age
Like great subterranean rivers.
And never before has humanity,
In such full consciousness,
Drifted towards so momentous
A moment in lived, measured time.
Minor spirits come out to play
And make mischief at Halloween
And on Walpurgis night.
Major spirits might be busy
In the slipstream of a new age.

So hold on to the best
Aspects of the awakened
Mind. For only the most solid
And intangible qualities
Of the human spirit can
Save us from succumbing
To the waves of panic
That will engulf us temporarily.

We need to be adaptive mariners.
But when the waves have passed,
When the silver line has been crossed,

And when we are safely over,
A new calm will descend on us.
A profound time change will settle
Upon us as we find ourselves
Not in a new land, but
In a new time,
In a new space.

At first we'll seem adrift
On a strange sea
Where fishes no longer
Resemble what they used to be,
Where we are no longer
What we once were,
Or what we thought we were.

And we'll have become less,
Or more,
Depending on what we
Have brought with us
From the old time,
From the old space.

Now's the moment to choose
What we're going to freight over.
We are going to need

Our sanity later.
It will have been tempered
And raised to such a pitch
That out of its higher power
Will come the next grand stage
Of the evolution
Of human consciousness.
Of a higher history.
The foundations of a
New universal civilisation.

SEVEN

No One is a Loser

I

Our future is greater
Than our past. So
Far we have mostly misapplied
The powers of the mind.
We have under-applied
The wonders of the human soul.
The mind that created pyramids,
Warfare, great art, science,
Has not yet reached maturity.
Everything we have done till now
Merely suggests
The power of the human
Mind in its infancy.

We're not defined by our failures.
And rivers have changed their courses.
There are revolutions in the heavens,
Among the stars, all the time.
New worlds are constantly being born.
What we call civilisation
Is only ten years old
In the mind of a palmer oak,
And a minute old
To a distant star.
Tradition doesn't have
To weigh us down.

We weigh ourselves
Down with tradition, with
The past, with past failures,
Past forms, past perceptions.
We've made these things.
And we can unmake them.
Every now and again the earth
Breaks its crust, and molten liquid
In its depths spews out,
Turns to rocks, and forms new islands.
The mind of humanity is such a force.
New worlds wait to be created by
Free minds that can dream unfettered,
Without fear, turning obstacles into
Milestones towards the luminous glories.
The new age is such a time for
Such new births. We
Can all re-dream the world, our lives,
But the conception must begin now.
The birth must begin now.
We ought to consecrate ourselves
To clearing the deadwood and stale thinking
And backward perceptions from our minds.
We should begin to think anew.
To prepare ourselves for a new
Air, for a fuller future.

The preparation would be rewarding,
For we're each one of us saviours
And co-makers of the world
We live in. But we should begin
Now, here, among
One another,
And in solitude.

II

We must not think ourselves victims,
Disadvantaged, held back –
Because of race, colour, or creed,
Education, class, or gender,
Religion, height, or age.
The world is not made of labels.
But the world, from now on,
Will be made through the mind.
Through great dreaming, greater loving
And masterly application.
Those who transcend their apparent limitations
Are greater than those who apparently
Have little to transcend.
Our handicaps can be the seed of our glories.
We shouldn't deny them. We
Should embrace them,
Yes, embrace our marginalisation,
Our invisibility, our powerlessness.
Embrace our handicaps, and then use them,
And go beyond them, for
They could well be the key
To some of the most beautiful energies
That we have been given.
Accept no limitation to the human potential.
We have the power of solar systems
In our minds.

Our rage is powerful
Our love too is mighty
Our desire to survive is tremendous.
Our quest for freedom is noble, and great.
Just as astonishing is the knowledge
That we are, more or less,
Makers of the future.
And we create what time will frame.
And a beautiful dream, shaped
And realised by a beautiful mind,
Is one of the greatest gifts
We can make to our fellow beings.

III

Never again will we stand on
The threshold of a new age. We
That are here now are touched
In some mysterious way
With the ability to change
And make the future. Those
Who wake to the wonder
Of this magic moment, who
Wake to the possibilities
Of this charged conjunction, are
The chosen ones who have chosen
To act, to free the future, to open it up,
To consign prejudices to the past,
Open up the magic casement
Of the human spirit
To a more shining world.

Then, a few centuries into the future,
The miseries and sufferings
Of continents will be rumours
Of contended history;
There will be no famines
And no mass starvations
No tolerance of tyranny.
Liberty will have a more glorious song.
And then humanity will spend

Time's repletion dreaming of ways
To use new freedoms and powers
Of the race for higher things,
Much as we find better uses
For electricity or solar energy.

EIGHT

Turn on your Light

I

Do I see you recoil from this vision?
Have we become so neck-deep in
Cynicism that we threaten the race
With ever-descending spiral
Of failure, inaction, and negativity,
Indifference, boredom, stupidity?
Cynicism only creates dead worlds;
Its symbol, devoid of beauty,
A dead land, where nothing grows.
That's not the smarter side
Of the human spirit (as some like to think),
But the smaller, meaner, and least attractive,
The most death-encouraging side,
And the least effective.

We are better than that.
We are greater than our despair.
The negative aspects
Of humanity are not the most real
And authentic;
The most authentic thing
About us is our capacity to create,
To overcome, to endure, to transform,
To love, and to be greater than our suffering.
We're best defined by the mystery
That we're still here, and can still rise

Upwards, still create better civilisations,
That we can face our raw realities,
And that we'll survive the greater despair
That the greater future might bring.

II

The new era's already here:
Here the new time begins anew.
The new era happens every day,
Every day is a new world, a
New calendar.
All great moments,
All great eras,
Are just every moment
And every day writ large.
Thousands of years
Of loving, failing, killing, creating,
Surprising, oppressing,
And thinking ought
Now to start to bear fruit,
To deliver their rich harvest.

But will you be at the harvest,
Among gatherers of new fruits?
Then you must begin today to remake
Your mental and spiritual world,
And join the warriors and celebrants
Of freedom, realisers of great dreams.

You can't remake the world
Without remaking yourself. Each
New era begins within. It

Is an inward event,
With unsuspected possibilities
For inner liberation. We
Could use it to turn on
Our inward lights.
We could use it to use
Even the dark and negative
Things positively. We
Could use the new era
To clean our eyes,
To see the world differently,
See ourselves more clearly.
Only free people can
Make a free world.
Infect the world
With your light. Help
Fulfil the golden prophecies.
Press forward the human genius.
Our future is greater than our past.

III

Already, the future is converging
With the past. Already
The world is converging.
The diverse ways of the world
Will create wonderful new forms,
Lovely cultural explosions
In the centuries to come.
Already I sense future forms of art,
Of painting, sculpture, and humour.
Already I sense future novels, plays,
Essays, poems, dances.
Already I sense the great orchestras
Of humanity, a world symphony,
A world jam, in which the diverse
Genius of the human race –
Its rich tapestry of differences –
Will combine, weave, heighten
Harmonise all its various ways
And bring about
A universal flowering
In all the vast numbers of disciplines,
Among the unnumbered peoples.
For already I can hear
This distant music of the future,
The magic poetry of time,
The distillation of all our
Different gifts.

It's all in the air
It's all gathering in
The underground
Coming together majestically.
We should listen to the things
Forming in the air,
The things forming
In the underground.
We should do some
Deep serious work
On the spirit of the age
If we're going to bring about
A marvellous future,
If we're going to have
Some control on
How the unknown
Will affect us.
The air must be altered,
And the underground must
Be understood,
For the overground to
Be different.

This distant music of
The future haunts me.

I think it will
Be something amazing
To hear,
A delight to the gods,
Provided we don't lose
Our way more than
We already have,
Provided we
Are guided by
Our deepest love,
The vast love that
Connects us all
On this little
Globe of beauty.

IV

And so because
We have too much
Information
And no clear
Direction;

Too many facts,
Not enough faith;
Too much
Confusion,
And craving clear
Vision;
Too many fears,
Not enough light –

I whisper to myself
Modest maxims,
Thought-friends
For a new age.

See clearly, think
Clearly.
Face pleasant and
Unpleasant truths;
Face reality.
Free the past. Catch

Up with ourselves.
Never cease from
Upward striving.
We're better than

We think.
Do not be afraid

To love, or be loved.
As within, so
Without.

We owe this life
Abundant happiness

V

Illusion of
Time will
Give way
To the reality
Of time…

And time
Present
Is made
Before
Time
Becomes
Present.

For all time is
Here, now,
In our

Awakening.

IV

For, after the gospels,
After human
And divine comedies,

And the one thousand and
One nights,
And after crime
And punishment,
War and peace, pride
And prejudice,
The sound
And the fury,

Between
Good and evil,
Being
And nothingness,
After the tempest, the trial,
The wake,
And the wasteland,
After things have

Fallen apart,
After the hundred years
Of solitude,
And the remembrance of

Things past,
In the kingdom
Of this world, in
Our time,

We can still astonish
The gods within humanity,
And be the stuff
Of future legends, if
We but dare to be real,
And have the courage to
See that this is the time

To dream the best
Dream of them all.